LATER THE HOUSE STOOD EMPTY

Dear Jo Ann,
Many Thanks for hearing my
reading. I'm glad to meet you
and hear about your word-work, too.
Best wishes,
Melina

LATER THE HOUSE STOOD EMPTY

Melina Draper

borealbooks

Book design and layout by Nicholas Smith

Cover design by Rebecca Buhler and Nicholas Smith

Library of Congress Cataloging-in-Publication Data

Draper, Melina, 1974–

[Poems. Selections]

Later the House Stood Empty / Melina Draper.——First edition.

pages cm

ISBN 978-1-59709-973-8 (paperback)

I. Title.

PS3604.R376A6 2014 811'.6—dc23

2013048735

The Los Angeles County Arts Commission, the National Endowment for the Arts, the Pasadena Arts and Culture Commission and the City of Pasadena Cultural Affairs Division, the Los Angeles Department of Cultural Affairs, Dwight Stuart Youth Fund, and Sony Pictures Entertainment partially support Red Hen Press.

First Edition

Published by Boreal Books

an imprint of Red Hen Press, Pasadena, CA

www.borealbooks.org

www.redhen.org

ACKNOWLEDGMENTS

Thank you to the editors in whose publications the following poems appeared, sometimes in different form: *Cimarron Review*, "El Oreja" and "Some gossip I would have liked to tell her"; *Crazyhorse*, "Coda"; *PALABRA: A Chicano and Latino Magazine of Literary Art*, "Aubade," under the title "Colonia," and "Mouth of the River"; *Extract(s)*, "Isabelle's Farm"; *ZYZZYVA*, "Don Carlos on Spanish Women" and "Terra Incognita."

Warm thanks to my family, teachers, friends, and readers, especially Brad Draper, Elena Lafert, Jorge Sarigiannis, Maritxu and Máximo Lafert, J. P. Fablet, Sebastián Rivero, Sergio Tarter, Daniel Barbeito, Cicely Buckley, Kevin Eib, Amber Flora Thomas, Derick Burleson, John Morgan, Gerri Brightwell, Charles Simic, Mekeel McBride, Nicole Stellon O'Donnell, Brooke Sheridan, Greg Lyons, Tom Moran, Amy Hartley, Gary Widger, Zia Dastoor, David Crouse, Peggy Shumaker, Jeanne Clark, and Alla Ivanchikova.

For Jorge and Elena

TABLE OF CONTENTS

LATER THE HOUSE STOOD EMPTY

Mouth of the River

Crackle and spit of fat on grills,
asado, chorizo in eucalyptus shade,
Fanta naranja, invasive foxtails waving.
I was a visitor in his country, too.

Like a foreign language, I learned him
lick by lick, his salty palms.
Scribbled into the world, our tall friend,
thin, like a cartoon, slipped away.
A bougainvillea spill of blossoms.
The plum tree practically family.

We made love in his hammock,
riding the waves of a whale's spine.
Umbilical river. Slow ocean feed.
Forty feet of vertebrae washed up
on shore. And later moving sands
exposed the tip of a dinosaur tail,
this story, and other bones.

I. Buenos Aires

Te sentía en los patios del Sur y en la creciente

Sombra que desdibuja lentamente

Su larga recta, al declinar el día.

Ahora estás en mí. Eres mi vaga

Suerte, esas cosas que la muerte apaga.

—Jorge Luis Borges, "Buenos Aires"

I felt you in the patios of the South and in the lengthening

Shadow that slowly erases

Its long line as day fades.

Now you are within me. You are my vague

Fortune, what death extinguishes.

TERRA INCOGNITA

Limestone wafers shelved like moldering books,
splintered centuries pressed into the continent's lip.
This *colonia* quaffed blood, ingested gristle, guts, and bone.

Into the mouth of the river the *vessel drove before her bows two billows of liquid phosphorus.*
Looking back, *the crest of every wave was bright.* The water, shook in a tumbler,
shot sparks. He found butterflies that clacked, their sound

similar to that of a toothed wheel passing under a spring catch.
And what of the stories he heard of the
marvelous property of certain rivers, which had the power of changing small bones into large,

of uprising Patagonia and Banda Oriental—where he found gigantic sloth
and armadillo-like animals entombed, a lost Pachydermata the size of a camel—
Carlos Darwin observed, *Formerly, it must have swarmed with great monsters.*

As the ancient maps suggested.

FLUVIAL DEPOSITS

this river, its tropical origin
somewhere north

i know because
it sweats piranhas
and snakes, red and black

still, the corner store man
swam its fifty-mile width

a *milonga* composed
to honor its name

people bound and gagged
dropped from planes
into its mouth

on clear days the city
winks on the horizon

ERYTHRINA CRISTA-GALLI

> . . . *llora sangre el ceibal* (the Ceibo weeps blood)
> —Aníbal Sampayo, "Río de los pájaros"

Anahí, queen of Guaraní
burned alive singing,
turned into the *Ceibo* tree
on the river's bank

where *desaparecidos* washed up.
Chinese ship-jumpers,
officials said, on account
of the eyes swollen shut.

The tree's red flowers
stick out their black tongues.

El Tigre

You could get lost in the Tigre Delta,
all the serpentine fingers
of the Paraná reaching
for the sea. The estuary lingers

so long, it takes them, as it takes
all, into itself, out of the heart
of the country. You could get lost
here among lugubrious mansions, art

deco, peeling lopsided decks
battered by the tidal pull of that siren
song moon and the Río de la Plata.
We've taken the back way in.

Rusted hulks bleed into the water—
ships' graveyard—tires buffer miles
of trash from our swale.
Not tropical enough for crocodiles.

Mosquitoes, plenty, and willows.
Painter Horacio Butler adored
El Tigre, its wilted decadence, the failed
amusement park, peeling and bored

around the final bend. My *tíos*
wave from the landing—
Buenos Aires teeming behind them.
Its dancers' legs are standing

on a swamp; its airs, the put-on kind.
The jungle's breath comes from upriver.
A violent, wet feeling. The move from
delta to city makes me shiver.

Heel Turns

Two men dancing cheek to cheek,
a dance so dirty, a woman won't be seen,
in La Boca, Buenos Aires, where bars speak

easy of booze, smoke, sex not too discreet.
Bordello next door. The scene:
two men dancing cheek to cheek,

sexy, weeping notes of *bandoneón*, a squeak
from black-heeled boots, turning sharp, clean,
in La Boca, Buenos Aires, where bars speak.

Gardel's smoky voice, his black hair sleek
with paste. Bodies long and lean—
two men dancing cheek to cheek.

Women, bare and daring, at last sneak
in to smoke, to dance the dance only seen
in La Boca, Buenos Aires, where bars speak

in code, turning two-four time. In a sultry pique,
the macho, slippery beats evoke the sweaty sheen
of two men dancing cheek to cheek
in La Boca, Buenos Aires, where bars speak.

GRANDE DAME

Rain comes in. Vines climb
the charred walls long after
the fire. She lets her son steal
coins from her purse, knows

he'll let some man give him a blow
for a sandwich or a few pills.
What tenuous thread,
she wonders, tethers them

to the canopy of each day?
A night-blooming cereus
invades the kitchen with its
carrion cologne. Snails

shellac the counter, their papery
traces etched in the lines
of her face. The city exacts
her price in daughters and sons.

Don Carlos on Spanish Women

An army captain asked:
Tell me, have you ever seen women

more beautiful than in Buenos Ayres?
Darwin assured him he had not,

and even agreed that their combs
were larger than those worn in Spain.

Writing home he said they were
angels gliding down the streets.

He said *involuntarily we groaned out,*
"how foolish English women are,

they can neither walk nor dress."
He said *how ugly Miss sounds*

after Signorita; I am sorry for you all;
it would do the whole tribe of you

a great deal of good
to come to Buenos Ayres.

EXCRETIONS

I went to visit a friend in the city.
His girlfriend had just had a late abortion.

We rode the bus to a rundown museum near the docks.
She cast a squint-eye at me as she kissed my friend.

Inside we contemplated the painting of a nude.
The girlfriend raised her arm, leaned in, and pressed

a daubed raspberry nipple. She reached to cup
her own breast, pulled away, leaving a wet spot.

Our eyes lingered, heavy, like her touch.
No one there to tell us what to do.

Crow's Nest

Yaya's apartment's a mansion
when I'm two, tunneling halls.
She lives eleven stories up, city
a dull roar below. Her cat hides

in the corridor, zaps my ankles as I pass
to the back where ancestors loom
in piled hair and frocks. At six I slip
between books packed tight

in Spanish, English, French.
A painting traps me, street angled
by the Basque great-great-grandfather
Elorriaga. And watch out for

the organics. Seeds explode into stars
if you touch them, a cone draws blood
from my fingertip, shells hum
the faraway sound.

At twelve—naked people among
the art books, Klimt, Rodin.
I see a skull on the windowsill
across the street near geraniums.

Underwear wave from rooftops.
On the street below, mornings, Pinky,
retired from the profession, does her
makeup in the doorway where she sleeps.

The Real News

One day Yaya saw a Russian satellite
perch on the rooftop across the street,

landing gear gleaming, sinister frame,
red spider-eyes spinning. It hummed.

Black smoke rolled up in fat tires. She couldn't
get through to anyone on the phone.

And when dinosaurs walked the streets
of Buenos Aires, she knew the end had come.

The newspapers failed to report it,
and Herodotus came to take her away.

On Blindness

Our hands shook,
our last meeting formal,

every gesture economized.
My grandfather pulled

a book from his shelf
to read me a poem by Borges,

about going blind. Something
about the penumbra.

He probably used the word
sepulchral. He read it aloud,

explained it. This was
the final message,

coded in my grandfather's
wincing speech.

I showed him stories I wrote.

He said, "Don't get fat."

On the wall in a photograph

from another time, we stand

close on the bow of a ship. Tonight,

I thumb through the *Obra poética*,

two dictionaries to my right,

still blind.

The Protest, 35 Years

Few mothers still march
around the Plaza de Mayo obelisk,
seeking who was taken from them,
who was disappeared.
Men with thick moustaches smoke,
sip tiny coffees, assert that the girl
Argentina, given the name
because her hair was silver and her skin
cast its own pale shimmer,
left freely on foot across the vineyards
of Mendoza into the Andes,
a place of prophecies,
where surely she must have acquired
a poncho to guard against the cold.
From there northward to, who knows?
Rain erases the circled treads
around the monument.
It might as well snow.

BIER

In a Pampean deposit, 1833, Darwin noted
a breccia of bones, gigantic osseous armor,
toxodon and mastodon teeth, and one of a horse,

now extinct. Think of its imported relatives
thriving among the gauchos and grass.
He heard of a drought so severe,

the mud banks of the Paraná trapped
thousands of desiccated cattle; a drought
that cycles through every fifteen years.

With prescience, he knew, as the grasslands
of the Pampas and Banda Oriental once rose,
so the estuary, fanning silt, would deliver bones.

II. The Other Side of the River

Tú sabes

que adivinan

el misterio:

me ven,

nos ven,

y nada

se ha dicho . . .

—Pablo Neruda

You know

they've guessed

our secret:

they see me,

they see us,

without saying a thing . . .

From the Barque

While Darwin, landlubber, explored escarpments
and thistle beds, magical rivers, deposits of bone,

Captain Robt. FitzRoy kept their berth.
Dear Philos (beloved), he wrote, excited by

the letter's skipping from ship to shore
across the river (*I never will write another letter after*

tea—that green beverage makes one tipsy—)
Beef for the crew, please, who are sounding

the depths, one lead weight overboard on a line
at a time; slow going to see what peaks

and valleys lie beneath. Creatures of the deep
appear in fossil, though not these; in jest,

he tells him they await his return *to assist*
in the parturition of a Megalonyx measuring seventy-two feet

from the end of his Snout to the tip of his tail—
and an Ichthyosaurus somewhat larger than the Beagle.—

Darwin, *avis in navibus rarissima*, not a strange bird,
but a rare one, greeny about the jowls when aboard,

striding happily on land, lamenting
the sorry skull used as target by the gauchos,

not seeking adventure, but finding it,
bringing it aboard in stories, wanting more.

Possession

She wanted it,
the gold ring engraved
with his name. It beckoned
like fate in her backyard.

As a boy he lost it
poking in the dirt.
Because love trumps
almost everything,

she gave it to me.
He whistled through his teeth
when he saw it, *Mirá!*
I would not give it to him.

It was a gift from his grandma
who raised him. I
wore it around my neck
on a chain as a devotion.

Aubade

At the end of the night I spiral
to the lighthouse top. The watchman
shares his bitter tea. Dawn alights
on the peninsula's pout, tips
church cupolas. Brushed cotton
wind whispers *aquí, aquí,*
cools my body's flush
from the bed of a lover
who called me *cachivache,*
mamarracho, as if I were
a crooked, inelegant mistake.

With fool's silver at sunup,
the river tricked us all to treasure.
Pirate here, caudillo there.
Brethren of Charrúa and Guaraní.
From here I see the elliptic cove,
barrancas pocked with caves,
forsythia tops spitting yellow.
Foreigners' yachts tethered
to the dock's crumbling edge,
empty buildings, graffiti that says
te amo. The pink wall of his house.

Convent ruins root the lighthouse,

where I descend in flutter

of pigeons' wings. Dogs lead

me through the Plaza Mayor,

between bearded, drunken

trees. I trip on tart oranges

neighbors gather for jam,

past museums housing cannonballs

children dug from their backyards.

Mist crooks and beckons from the river.

Spitshine

Moths and beetles court the street lamp on the corner.
I sit there into the wee hours writing.
I am his *sweet bitter unmanageable creature*,
jasmine-scented apparition *who steals into* his loft late.
He kisses me hard, he pinches me.
Love-salt distills.
By morning, I've grown tall, tall, my shadow says.
My skin is freshly peeled, my mouth is bruised.
The cobblestones are wet and citrus scented.
A jacaranda flings trumpet blossoms to the ground, purple fog.
Any minute now I will rise up and fly above the town.

BEFORE THE CONFESSION

Sneaking home, I saw
it dressed (or
undressed?) in silver
by the dawn. Silt

drawn down
from the Paraná mixes
with the Uruguay come from
the jungle, spilling

into the moody Río
de la Plata.
Pulled this way
and that by the moon, it

will lose itself
into blue and salt,
soon. I turn my back
to its blushing.

The skeleton key barks once,
twice. The heavy door opens
into my stepfather's
raised brow.

OASIS

The hermit's moth-eaten cat
tied to a pole, straining and mewing

for touch, for food. The hermit asks
was I the girl from Tarariras. I wasn't.

I watch my lover slicing tomatoes.
He adds oil and vinegar, salt, says,

That's how the juices come out, see.
Because I am young, he teaches me.

I memorize his bluish lips,
his nip. His smile, like the hermit's,

reveals spaces. The men talk,
I practice silence, hidden in the palace

made of driftwood and rushes
at the foot of the cliff.

You are not so different, the river says,
who prefer to be alone.

The Bullring

We snuck into the Plaza de Toros,
still grand. Blood in its ground.
Crepitant walls crumbling.
He told me he loved me.

Smell of horses wafting on the breeze.
Nickering. He asked me to stay
with him. Outside the bullring
the acacia dropped its thorns.

I knew where the green parrots nestled.
I pressed his ring, a baby ring
with his name engraved on it, into
his hand. *Please*, he begged, *keep the ring*.

After I knew a woman

I knew a man, lovely in his bones,
when a tomcat yowled, he took it in;
ah, when he moved, I sighed and moaned—
how flesh alone? and skeleton?—
(it was not his mind that drew me).
Blason! Blason! I need Shakespeare to decree
his beauty from moustache to knee.

He knew the value of aesthetics
in wooing women: bait and wait.
He taught me the night is for athletics;
oh the ways a body can gyrate!
(Love came too late, when we were done.)
In the end it's he who intones,
I knew a woman, lovely in her bones.

SUNFLOWER WEAVE

Awash in ochre, the field and I.
I talk to a man lying next to me.
Wick green smell, like weeds just pulled.
In the dream, he always lies next to me.

We can't make love, I say.
Undulating disks in a gold sea.
Whose legs, soft and warm?
The sun takes us for awhile.

Thick leaves cloak my face.
Wreathed heads full of seeds.
Far away, something rings.
The man means nothing to me, I say.

Recurring Dream

Sunflowers turn their heads
as we hiccup by in the motorcar,

steam spewing across the hood.
Flying insects with guitars disappear

into a thicket. Parrots scatter in green
spray. Rotting ears of corn on dying stalks say

something I fear but do not understand.
I ignore the leggy wild artichokes.

The driver leans to kiss me, but I slip out,
tucking the baby armadillo under my arm.

The Guest

How I loved watching naked
from his narrow bed,
the dim light casting shadows
onto the whitewashed wall.

Late, after sweeping, he
locked the door, made
a motion with his head
to climb the ladder to the loft.

Alone, I peeked under the bed.
Dust bunnies, hairs, a letter
I'd sent, read and lost.
The oily strip of a condom.

BEHELD

I am tired of walking through the old barrio.

All the Portuguese stone alleys descend to the river.

When the rain comes down, I duck into the photographer's studio.

An orange tom watches water running down the panes.

Le digo Chatrán, says the man.

I make a note to remember this forever.

In a few minutes the man takes a picture of my hairy leg up close.

From the darkroom he tells me to drink some *mate*.

Ear torn and dusty, the cat purrs when I scratch its head. *Chatrán*.

I feel I could stay here.

Like a stray come home.

The man shows me the photograph.

The rain stops and the sun streams in.

Before I leave, I ask to see it once more.

Winter mountain dotted with black spruce.

His demeanor suggests I am beautiful.

III. Ghosts

¿De qué desierto antiguo eres memoria
que tienes sed y en agua te consumes
y alzas el cuerpo muerto hacia el espacio
como si tu agua fuera la del cielo?
—Alfonsina Storni, "Río de la Plata en arena pálido"

From which ancient desert do you come, memory,
thirsty, consuming yourself in water
and flinging your dead body toward space
as if your water belonged to the sky?

CONFLUENCE

for Alfonsina

The estuarine river ebbs and flows,
coquettish in silver,
turbulent and dolorous in brown.
It eddies round me, child, woman, song,
as it did her, croaking invite,
silent witness, fanning sediment
and phytoplankton visible
only from above and ago.
Somewhere at its mouth
it braids with blue and salt, becomes
foreign to itself, and something else.

There she wrote her last poem,
just before the sea, hymn to a mother.
Rock me, love me, she said, croon me a rhyme,
moss for my pillow, lamp by my head,
any constellation will do. You choose.

Two Voices

A week after she died, the postman pushed her letter through the slot.
I hear tell there used to be a lonely royal girl like me upon a time.
What she sought, what she meant, I could not know.
The taste of dance is on my tongue, my hair is loose,
she wrote. Threads of stories set thrumming.
There is yet one, her tears stitch gleaming pearls all night.
There is yet one, I say. I am she, who waits.
Under every leaf have I looked. The lanes, the secret nooks.
Now, I look for her in Meera's poems. She says,
A moment without you is no moment.
I wait for a sign from god or ghost that does not come.
To love one not earthly this is the root of pain, my friend,
she says. Mourning, I make a list of elegant things.
Says Meera, I count the stars, I wait for one pin of light.

The Suicide

Pitito knew words from thirteen languages.
He worked the docks,

earned coins for gallantry,
for carrying tourists' bags and playing

host with bow and nod. Old wino,
his smile caught you.

It was an act, a kind of work
that masked the daily

pain of penury and shame.
My mother fed him now and then,

the holy fool. She'd known him
as the only hippie back in the day,

long braid down his back, and guitar.
He'd been a ship's hand, too.

He showed me his collection
of business cards, evidence of friends

from Russia, Germany, Japan. He had
a gun, a missing thumb, a son.

Someone found him in his bed,
a ring of blood pooled around his head.

Later the House Stood Empty

The river never so big.
Someone whispered Brazil.
Someone suicide. Foul play.
Friends combed marsh, hill,

and thicket. Someone said AIDS.
His sweet house, his mother
gaunt and diminished, at the door
mistook me for another.

I knocked once in the wee
hours to fetch him to the water,
each of us expecting the other
to bring the pole. The patter

of fishermen in caps, cats
bald and meowing—we listened
and talked and dreamed
as the sailboats listed.

The Gift

Maria took me for kind and wise
in my wide-eyed foreigner silence.
It's true I let my gaze linger
on her features. It's true
some gazes feel like a caress.

She told me her story while I
took in her long dark hair
woven with silver in the garden light,
eyes kalamata-bruised,
darting left to right, her hand

warm in mine. She worked hard
despite her failing body, mind
that would not keep steady.
Winter nights her house was cold
next to the river, where an old girlfriend

let her stay out of pity or obligation.
Before she died she gave me—
in gratitude, for listening—
an earthen pot, rustic, mud-made.
Too fragile to carry with her.

THEY LOVED THE SEA AND THE SYMBOL OF THE SEA

They made a pact, the two friends,
when the time came,
to take a boat, sail away, and die.

One grew ill.
His friend reminded him,
Let's go, he said, *I'm ready.*

Did they go?
Yes. In a small wooden boat to the vast.
Yes. To be cleansed by saltwater and eaten by fishes.

Andate a la mierda, said the sick man.
The problem of the failing body.
As it turned out, the idea had been about living.

After the Call

The night and I grew faint.
If I slept I would lose her.
Already she was gone.

How the concavity of her eyes
like eaves drew shadows to rest.
Blue tints in hair and skin.

Supple and languid,
in motion and in repose,
clothed and nude.

Her laugh, a seal's bark,
full-body shake. I craved
its sound as I forgot it.

Honeysuckle scent wafting
on the breeze. I thought
we had all time.

Come morning, I kept her
wrapped around me
like a cowl.

SOME GOSSIP I WOULD HAVE LIKED TO TELL HER

Far from home, mid-river,
three hours to cross on the slow ferry,
I spotted the boy we'd known.

What a small world, I said. He did not
smile, but nodded, angling his whole body
toward his dapper friend. When I told him

about the accident, how she died,
he said he did not remember her,
even though she'd desired him.

(She'd said it, nostrils quivering, bangles
jingling, white-collared shirt tightening
against her tangerine breasts.)

About this, I said nothing. It appeared
he was in love with his companion
and did not remember me, either.

El Gato

He walked barefoot through town,
brandishing the gun like a lunatic cowboy,
out into the grassy shallows of the bay
toward the beach lined with trees that drop
foul-smelling seeds shaped like black ears.
Something like mercy helped him vanish
into the thick *juncos* and cane.

Years later, I saw him, delivering pizzas strapped
to the back of a moped, clean-shaven and perfumed.

POVERTY AND ABUNDANCE

Arms muscled and lean,
hands gloved in powder, she
winds potato dough into snakes,
dices, rolls each *ñoqui* down fork tines
for texture, boils to float, and serves
them steaming with the rabbit
she pulled from the hatch that morning,
skinned, and fried. She ladles
portions, flour in her hair.
Rabbit again? a child whines.
Tomorrow there will be more.
No word from the patriarch
chewing at the head of the table,
glass eye staring left.

Footnote

The cacique fled the slaughter, no bridle,
no saddle, arm around the horse's neck,
leg slung over its back, body hanging down
to one side, son bundled in his other arm.

The commandant changed horses three times and failed!
marveled the soldiers at the pass at Cholechel.
All cheer for the one who gets away. *What a fine*
picture, Darwin wrote, *the naked, bronze-like figure*

of the old man with his little boy riding like a Mazeppa
on the white horse, thus leaving far behind him
the host of his pursuers! Cossacks, steppes invoked.
Entombed in the book, he's inspiration, exculpation,

history's mezzanine. Ground-truth,
small town named for Darwin upstream.

Panoramic (Darwin and Me)

I'm seventeen. He's twenty-four,
set to sail round the Horn
through the Strait of Magellan,
months from the Galapagos birds,
twenty years from *Origin of Species.*
Though what to make of the story
of Earth in evidence of sea on land?
What of these remains of *mollusca*—
whose relatives still live offshore,
while others are nowhere else found?
He walked across the land I call home,
to net, pickle, pack, ship, in service to
Science, Captain, and Queen.
His letters name the places I love,
and when he is tired of it and ready
to move away from that *stupid,*
unpicturesque side of America,
I forgive him. No revenge
in knowing what's to come.
He's still a century away from the throng
of millions of Spanish and Italians,
my great-great-grandfather among them,
two centuries from native population
three percent, though Rosas's killing has begun:

There is now carrying on a bloody war
of extermination against the Indians.
This inheritance I do not want to own.

IV. Coda

También el árbol sin moverse estaba

y el pájaro lejano y le escribían

delgadas nubes la palabra Espero.

—Alfonsina Storni, "Río de la Plata en gris áureo"

And the tree stood motionless,

and the far bird, and threadlike clouds

wrote the words *I await you.*

El Oreja

I returned to that town.
The street dogs had been poisoned,
and the man I loved no longer
lived on the street of sighs.
Nights I roamed for him.
A rumor whispered he was dodging cops
by the shore. A willow trailed
into the river near the old fortress.
I came upon the grave
of a dog beloved of the townspeople.
A photo wrapped in plastic,
painted on the wall the words
Oreja, el mejor de los perros.
I knew him, too, a large male
with proud balls, wandering alone.
He used to sun himself
in the convent ruins with other dogs.
That place, now empty,
smelled of moss and piss.

CRACKED

The farmhouse tucked beside the copse.
Trees rattle and wheeze, laurel, lemon,
bamboo, oak, and eucalyptus. "Fall," he thinks,
but no, it's summer. A snake-long choke-hold
seca is cycling through or here to stay.
Whole trees have died or shed their leaves.
His life is measured by the orchard's hush.
Three shriveled plums steal sweetness from
another year. The oven bird has fled her home.
A meter-stick probes for moisture, pokes into dust.
A rabbit flees, the dog gives chase. Her fox tail wags
as spittle drips. Her thirst, unlike the unslaked earth's,
is vital. Silver trickles from the hose, small jewels,
but not enough. Nothing left to do but dance.

Marcela

Door to door *el yuyero* peddles
bouquets. He's been out in *el campo*
gathering the yellow blooms.
His hands, his hat, his hut, perfumed

with drying flowers hung from rafters.
Door to door, *Marcela?* he asks,
a girl's name, like Lily or Rose.
Picked at its peak under a full moon.

Plugs ulcers, shrinks stones, brings
blood, makes wishes come true.
A certain photographer always buys
a bunch, pinches off the heads

of three dried flowers, adds them
to the *mate* water. I sip. It carries me
to the field, untamed, beyond
the town. Bitter, but good.

Girl, 9, Runs Errand

Take jug. Take coin. Lug jug.
Half block. Half block.
Cobblestone, cobblestone.
Squint in. *Almacén.*

Hola Doña Cucaracha.
Bad teeth. Loose grin.
Fill the *damajuana, por favor.*
Bubble-glub, glub, glub.

Sharp, red, pungent sting.
Coin give. Take jug.
Lug jug. Cobble-wobble.

Stone step. Door ajar.
Sizzle-shh, onions fry.
Vino home. *Gracias, amor.*

Bon Voyage

At sundown in a copper bowl, she lights
an echo of the sun with ghee, hums
Agnaye Svaha. Agnaye idam na mama.
Prajapataye Svaha. Prajapataye idam na mama,

and throws in rice. From the balcony, her mind
wanders into the mulberry. Branch by branch
she creeps to the river, dips in a toe, rolls
on wavelets to the horizon, the city, north

across the continent she walked at twenty,
past glaciers, mountains, jungle, desert,
she moves among the dead and living.
The cow dung sputters, sparks, scents

the house with smoke. The sun's set. She rises,
ignoring cobwebs laced in the stairwell,
dust motes dancing underfoot,
to cook vegetables for her hungry daughter.

Strange Like Me

In the courtyard, first day of school
in Uruguay, I'm nine, dizzy
epicenter of a circle widening round me,

the first American girl specimen
they've seen. I'm tall and strange
like the sycamores lining

the four blocks to school
in spots and spores.
In class, seated short to tall,

I watch their heads.
Recess means *mate cocido*,
sweet and green, *mortadella*

on bread, Marcelo running,
long in the torso and blond.
When the Norwegian boy comes,

I take note, pass by his house
time and again until
report card day, his fist pump,

whoop, such joy at one
sobresaliente more than me,
in grammar.

TRAVELER

He's bored by hillocks and league after league of plains
undulating like the sea *but without its beautiful colour.*

Days here and there brightened by skeletons, one
nearly complete giant sloth, *scelidotherium*—but he yearns

for the jungle, the Amazon, its *magic*, color more than
dun, more than *ever the muddy estuary of the Plata.*

He wants spring at home instead of in October,
his garden *paradise*, he'd like to be there now,

like a *ghost* among his family. But he's proud:
I am become quite a Gaucho, drink my Mattee & smoke my cigar,

& then lie down & sleep as comfortably with the Heavens
for a Canopy as in a feather bed. It is such a fine healthy life.

(When the weather is nice.) He likes the *throat-cutting*
gauchos, *half wild, half Indian*, with their brightly colored

ponchos, how they eat nothing but meat caught
in the day, deer or ostrich, trapped *by throwing two balls,*

which are attached to the ends of a thong,
so as to entangle their legs, or eggs, sixty-four collected

in one day. See how they start a fire by rubbing twigs
into fibers, forming a nest to catch the wind and the flame,

how they feed their fire with bones from the feast, and how
he too is now a *gran galopeador*, traveling from Posta to Posta

(with a guide), Río Negro to Buenos Ayres, *a long journey*
between 500 & 600 miles, through a district, till very lately

never penetrated except by the Indians & never
by an Englishman, his luggage only a *Hammer Pistol,*

shirt, & *the Recado (saddle) makes the bed.*
Back at Monte Video, he awaits the *Beagle*

to carry him south to Tierra del Fuego,
braces for months of no letters.

Specimens packed and shipped,
he carries nothing but words.

Isabelle's Farm

Her big feet, bare
among the chickens.
All legs and belly,
she scatters feed.
Her two girls,
eyes and halos,
gather eggs.

Canvas stretched
to show the dream,
she paints: horse, womb,
fetus, terra cotta hands,
ochre smoke, and
her husband,
the blue goat.

The tomatoes fail,
and the egg business.
Her hands shape a living
from pottery lined blue.
The other brushes set aside,
canvasses stacked
behind a door.

On hot days she floats

naked in the water tank

above the empty granary.

Small Town Ghosts

parked in their Citroën
the Peiranos drink *mate,*
wrapped in coats and scarves

Rosita sweeps leaves
from the cobblestone street

my brother draws a portrait
of Victor in his studio,
cigarettes near shrunken hands

the dogs know what day
the butcher's meat arrives

the barrio *panadería*
where my grandfather bought *cuernitos*
also no longer exists

R*ETORNO*

The church is new. Don Carlos
saw the ruin of the old one
blown to bits. Full of powder,

struck by lightning, it lit good.
What new ruin is this,
stout walls cordoned off,

half-buried near the new church,
bridges linking me from here
to there? Bar across the street.

Hibiscus on the path.
The church is full of old people.
Who remembers me says

and where is your brother?
your brother? your brother?
Last time I walked here

this was not a store. The girl
who snuck around at night like me
still lives here. I saw her growing old.

The photographer's companion's new.
I wave and smile, wave
and smile, wave and smile.

POINT TO POINT

Among these sycamores
I played hide-and-seek

In the old fortress, there,
the whale skeleton extended

There, on that branch, two parrots
groomed a third, beaks buried in down

In that window framed by blossoms,
a woman wept to tangos

Beneath that doorway
my hundred love letters flew

CODA

How do the Aymara conceive
of the future behind, the past ahead?
A woman gestures with her arm

forward, meaning yesterday, last year.
What she knows is what she's seen.
I squint to see the past ahead.

Tomorrow, unknown, is behind me.
What a relief not to
anticipate it. I am surrounded

by the past, plural like old friends,
a disagreement or two still
festering. Toppled buildings stand

in shadow where they were.
Look, my friend's mother's at the door.
He's not there, is there

batting Nescafé to a froth.
We are at the pier wishing for *mate*.
I like me there, there, and there.

I can see us sitting,
our legs dangling down
against the rocks.

NOTES

Charles Darwin quotes, which appear as italics in the poems, are from Charles Darwin's *The Voyage of the Beagle* or The Darwin Correspondence Project, letters dated July 1833 to June 1834, retrieved from http://www.darwinproject.ac.uk/home.

The sunset mantra in "Bon Voyage" comes from an Agnihotra purification ritual for the atmosphere, originating in Hindu communities. Nonsectarian modern versions of the ritual are practiced for healing and purification. The Sanskrit translates as "Unto the fire I am offering all. This offering is not mine it is Thine."

Italicized lines in "Poem in Two Voices" are from *In the Dark of the Heart: Songs of Meera*, translated by Shama Futehally (New York: HarperCollins, 1994) from poems 3, 12, 18, 19, and 27, on pages 47, 69, 93, 97, and 121.

Epigraphs are translated by the author and taken from the following sources:
Jorge Luis Borges, *Obra poética.* (Buenos Aires: Emecé Editores, 1977), 272.
Pablo Neruda, "Oda al secreto amor," in *Obras completas*, 2nd ed. (Buenos Aires: Editorial Losada, 1957), 1245.
Alfonsina Storni, "Río de la Plata en arena pálido," in *Antología poética.* (Buenos Aires: Editorial Losada, 1998), 225.
Alfonsina Storni, "Río de la Plata en gris áureo," in *Antología poética.* (Buenos Aires: Editorial Losada, 1998), 224.

The poem "Spitshine" works off of a line from Sappho translated by Anne Carson: *sweetbitter creature who manages to steal in.*

ABOUT THE AUTHOR

Melina Draper's poems have appeared in *ZYZZYVA*, *Cimarron Review*, *Borderlands: Texas Review*, *PALABRA: A Magazine of Chicano & Latino Literary Art*, *Salamander*, and other journals. Her book *Place of Origin/Lugar de Origen* (Oyster River Press, 2008), co-authored with her mother, Argentine writer Elena Lafert, won the Latino Book Award for Best Bilingual Book of Poetry in 2009. She holds an MFA in poetry from the University of Alaska Fairbanks and an MA in fiction from the University of New Hampshire. She lives in Geneva, New York.